Honey Badgers

Julie Murray

Abdo Kids Junior
is an Imprint of Abdo Kids
abdobooks.com

Abdo
INTERESTING ANIMALS
Kids

abdobooks.com

Published by Abdo Kids, a division of ABDO, P.O. Box 398166, Minneapolis, Minnesota 55439.

Printed in the United States of America, North Mankato, Minnesota.

102022

012023

THIS BOOK CONTAINS RECYCLED MATERIALS

Photo Credits: Alamy, Getty Images, Minden Pictures, Shutterstock

Production Contributors: Teddy Borth, Jennie Forsberg, Grace Hansen

Design Contributors: Candice Keimig, Pakou Moua

Library of Congress Control Number: 2022937173

Publisher's Cataloging-in-Publication Data

Names: Murray, Julie, author.

Title: Honey badgers / by Julie Murray

Description: Minneapolis, Minnesota : Abdo Kids, 2023 | Series: Interesting animals | Includes online resources and index.

Identifiers: ISBN 9781098264154 (lib. bdg.) | ISBN 9781098264710 (ebook) | ISBN 9781098264994 (Read-to-Me ebook)

Subjects: LCSH: Honey badger--Juvenile literature. | Badgers--Juvenile literature. | Animals--Juvenile literature. | Zoology--Juvenile literature.

Classification: DDC 599.767--dc23

Table of Contents

Honey Badgers

Honey badgers live in Africa and Asia.

North America
Europe
Asia
Africa
South America
Australia
N
W
E
S

They are found in deserts and grasslands.

The honey badger has a thick body. Its legs are short.

It has a long nose.

Its teeth are sharp!

Honey badgers have white and black hair.

They have thick, **rubbery** skin. This protects them!

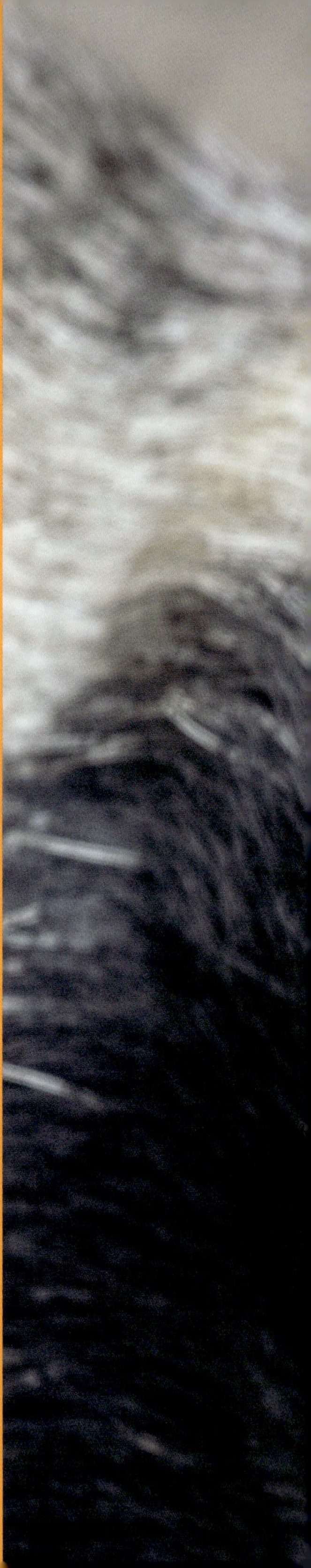

They are strong and **fierce**! They can take on much larger animals.

They have sharp claws.

They dig **burrows**.

They eat insects and snakes.

Their favorite food is honey!

Honey Badger Features

black and white hair

long nose

sharp claws

short legs

Glossary

burrow
a hole or tunnel dug by some animals for use as a hiding place or home.

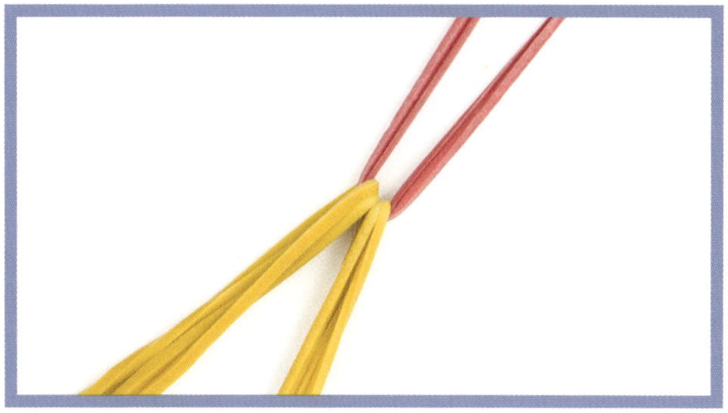

fierce
wild and dangerous; extremely intense.

rubbery
like rubber in feel and stretch.

Index